Teacher's Notes

Hallelujah Handel!

Based on the original work
by Douglas Cowling

Teacher's Notes written
by Susan Hammond

To Sarah and Katie,
who inspired this series

Published by The Children's Group Inc.
1400 Bayly Street, Suite 7
Pickering, Ontario, Canada L1W 3R2
For a complete catalogue, please call 1-800-757-8372
or e-mail moreinfo@childrensgroup.com
Visit us online at http://www.childrensgroup.com

Printed in Canada

CONTENTS

LETTER TO TEACHERS

Many teachers and young listeners have expressed their enjoyment of the Classical Kids recording *Vivaldi's Ring of Mystery.* Although *Hallelujah Handel!* is the sequel to that story, it also stands alone as a colorful depiction of Georgian London. This compelling story, about a young boy who sings but does not speak, is ultimately a tale about the healing power of music.

What really catches the imagination of a child first entering the world of classical music? We may never know, but the answer lies somewhere in a young listener's uncanny ability to paint pictures in his or her mind. To help in that process, Classical Kids gives careful attention to the music, biographical anecdotes and period sound effects, all within the framework of an emotional fictional story.

For classical music, the 18th century was a miracle, a musical feast! It began in Italy, where Vivaldi spun his concerti into the canals of Venice. Seven years later in 1685, just a few miles apart, Bach and Handel were born. While Bach remained in Germany to fill its churches and courts with unparalleled music, Handel traveled to England where he flooded public gardens and opera houses with magnificent choral and instrumental works. Imagine — in one lifetime, a child could study in Vivaldi's Pietà, meet Handel in London, enjoy the debut of Mozart's *The Magic Flute* in 1791 and even hear Beethoven's early symphonies!

Today, Georgian England holds a particular fascination for us. Movies compete to capture its elegant exteriors and dark inner madness. Behind these images streams Handel's music: his famous Sarabande, Water Music, Royal Fireworks Music and, of course, *Messiah.*

Ah yes, Handel's *Messiah.* Like Beethoven's Ninth Symphony, the story of its composition and reception almost equals the music itself. *Hallelujah Handel!* centers on the performance that finally earned Messiah its acceptance in England: the 1750 benefit concert for the Foundling Hospital. In what must be music history's greatest gift, Handel donated the score of his masterpiece to the orphans of London.

With those orphans lies the historical "hook" for *Hallelujah Handel!* Children are endlessly fascinated by those whose past is ripe with menace and possibility. They find comfort in the idea of spirit guardians who watch over their charges. It is this potent mixture of orphans, evil keepers and benevolent spirits that creates the fictional element in *Hallelujah Handel!*

But in the end, as always, it is the music that endures. Let the great Beethoven have the last word:

"Handel is the greatest composer that ever lived... I would uncover my head and kneel down at his tomb."

Susan Hammond

How This Book Is Organized

Classical Kids recordings have been used in K–9 classes, but are most suitable for Grades K to 6. We have ranked the activities according to grade level with the symbols below. The icon applies to all the activities in the section, unless otherwise indicated. In the Exploring the Music sections, the icon also includes a number indicating the appropriate National Standard for Arts Education (see page 5).

 K–2  3–4  5–6  3–6  All

Presenting the Recording

This recording can be presented in its entirety (approximately 45 minutes), in two halves or in the six scenes outlined here. Each scene is identified in terms of tape time elapsed, CD track numbers and beginning and ending dialogue. You will find in these Teacher's Notes:

Getting ready: Questions and activities for use before the recording

Scene-by-scene suggestions: For use during the recording
- The story
- Music used in the scene
- Interesting background facts
- Discussion and activity suggestions
- Suggestions for exploring the music

Follow-up: Questions and activities for use after the recording
- Charts: Themes and skills, and a 10-day lesson plan
- Student's worksheet

Music in the Integrated Curriculum

Although Classical Kids recordings can be enjoyed as musical stories, our aim is to move children from being passive listeners to active participants: to engage their imaginations, to offer new skills and knowledge, to stimulate higher-order thinking skills and, finally, to give every teacher the tools to build a rich learning environment. These Teacher's Notes present more than 70 facts and thought-provoking questions to move beyond music into an integrated curriculum of social studies, creative writing, math, sciences and the other arts.

Our intent is to provide both specialists and general classroom teachers with engaging materials that expand their students' knowledge of music and times past. Instead of presenting a basal text of sequential musical skills, Classical Kids urges teachers and their students to "play with" musical concepts, to develop an interpretive vocabulary, to sing or play classical melodies on simple classroom instruments, to write lyrics, even to venture into composition. Children find it difficult to work in a vacuum, so let these recordings serve as a model, captivating young listeners with a moving story and then motivating them to acquire new facts and skills. Put these recordings in your classroom library for repeated listening.

Classical Kids and Children with Special Needs

Classical Kids recordings do not talk down to children. Our challenge here has been to design concrete activities that are sufficiently broadly based to inspire and involve children with special needs.

Teachers of children with learning disabilities often use the activities designed for younger classes, or allow more time for tasks: retell the story, dance, draw, sing or clap. Those teaching children with physical disabilities concentrate on singing, storyboarding, drawing or discussing events from the past. Teachers of children who are deaf or hard of hearing can tell the compelling story of Beethoven's triumph over deafness in *Beethoven Lives Upstairs*.

ESL students benefit from recordings that use well-spoken English to promote oral comprehension. Singing and writing lyrics are also wonderful ways to learn a second language. Classical Kids materials are available in other languages. Illustrated books of *Beethoven Lives Upstairs* and *Tchaikovsky Discovers America* are available in Spanish, and recordings of *Beethoven Lives Upstairs* and *Vivaldi's Ring of Mystery* are available in French.

The Teacher's Notes in this series encourage gifted students to write variations, study rondo structure, venture into European history and write time-travel stories with shifting points of view.

To all students, we encourage you to ask: "Who would want to do the possible all your life? The *impossible* — that's exciting!"

Assessment

Assessment in the arts is always difficult, often subjective, yet ultimately essential to spur excellence. Depending on what you hope to achieve with your arts program, you can test students individually or in groups, orally or on paper, for skills or understandings. These Notes encourage children to form their own questions, define tasks, discover research strategies, justify interpretations and then create a final product. Each of these stages can be assessed by the teacher. A sample student worksheet is included at the end of this book.

Observe and assess your students not only on final results but also on the care taken with the process. We encourage specialists to move beyond traditional music skills into cultural history, creative writing, research projects, time lines, story boards, set designs, murals or dance. Conversely, general classroom teachers are urged to try musical activities not necessarily based on playing proficiency. These listening and interpretive skills are important for music and for life in general.

Exploring the Music with Classical Kids

The suggested activities in the Exploring the Music sections are coded by number to reflect how they fulfill the U.S. National Standards for Arts Education.

1. *Singing, alone and with others, a varied repertoire of music.* Classical Kids believes that singing is primary for all music-making. The series offers more than 40 classical songs written out, and students are encouraged to write their own lyrics to well-known orchestral pieces and sing them.
2. *Performing on instruments, alone and with others, a varied repertoire.* These Teacher's Notes offer more than 50 pieces written out for recorders, glockenspiels, piano or guitar.

3. *Improvising melodies, variations and accompaniments.* The series encourages actively "playing with" musical elements, making answering phrases in ABA form, creating melodies based on chords and scales, and improvising variations or canons.
4. *Composing and arranging music within specified guidelines.* Be it creating "music from Neptune," writing ragtime, superimposing melodies, or composing music over which to read script, we seek to fire a child's musical imagination.
5. *Reading and notating music.* All the written-out pieces can be photocopied for classroom reading. Some titles include step-by-step descriptions for learning to read notation.
6. *Listening to, analyzing and describing music.* Musical terminology, instrumentation and form are explained. We encourage students to graph the "musical spine" of scenes in terms of tempo, instrumentation and mood. Classical Kids is particularly interested in helping students develop a descriptive vocabulary to interpret and listen to music imaginatively.
7. *Evaluating music and music performances.* All the music on the recordings has been expressly recorded to reflect images in the script. This provides an opportunity to talk about the performances and compare them to other recordings of the same piece.
8. *Understanding relationships between music and the other arts as well as disciplines outside the arts.* Classical Kids offers something unique for the last two criteria (8 and 9). The Discussion and Activities sections link music to other arts and subjects.
9. *Understanding music in relation to history and culture.* In the Background section of every scene, the music is set in its historical context. You will find a wealth of anecdotal facts and vivid descriptions of the times, without having to go to a library for outside sources.

(Adapted from National Standards for Arts Education *published by Music Educators National Conference. Copyright 1994. Reproduced with permission. The complete National Standards and additional materials related to the standards are available from Music Educators National Conference, 1806 Robert Fulton Drive, Reston, VA 22091.)*

Synopsis of the Story

In 1750, Handel gave musical history's greatest gift — his *Messiah* — to an orphanage in London. From that city's dark lanes comes Thomas, a boy who sings like an angel but will not speak. Finally, the boy is healed with the help of Maestro Handel, Katarina (from *Vivaldi's Ring of Mystery*), and the power and glory of the music.

Things to Talk About Before the Recording

Hallelujah Handel! can be enjoyed on its own or as a sequel to *Vivaldi's Ring of Mystery*.

- Listen to the Vivaldi recording to introduce Younger Katarina to your class. Like Thomas, she was an orphan. After studying with Vivaldi in Venice, she was united with her grandfather, who took her to England. There she met Handel and Thomas, the starting point for *Hallelujah Handel!*
- The Classical Kids recording *Mr. Bach Comes to Call* is another good story to pair with *Hallelujah Handel!* Both Handel and Bach were born in the year 1685, seven years after Vivaldi in Venice.

- *Hallelujah Handel!* is about a boy who sings but does not speak. Can anyone name books or movies that involve a silent child? [Suggestions: *Amazing Grace and Chuck, Tommy*.]
- This recording features a spirit mother and choir. What books or movies feature guardian angels? [Suggestions: *Angels in the Outfield, It's a Wonderful Life, Into the West*.]
- Ask students if they think there are forces of good and evil at work in the world? Do spirits watch over us?
- Handel's music is used in many movies and commercials today. Play some excerpts from the Hallelujah Chorus, the Hornpipe in D or the famous Sarabande in D Minor. Does anyone recognize these pieces? Do they know who wrote them? Where have they heard them?
- Georgian England holds a great fascination for us. Ask your students to imagine they are living 300 years ago. How might life be different? How would people travel in Georgian England? Dress? Eat? Entertain themselves?
- Have any of your students seen movies set in Georgian England (e.g., *The Madness of King George*)? Can they describe the images from Handel's times?
- There is a wonderful opera scene in *Hallelujah Handel!* In preparation for this segment, ask your class:
  - Has anyone been to an opera? What was its name, story and setting?
  - What is the difference between an opera and a musical? [Answer: Operas feature mostly song, are often in other languages; musicals have more spoken dialogue, are most frequently presented in English.]
  - Give some examples of each. [Answers: Operas — Mozart's *The Magic Flute*, Handel's *Julius Caesar*, Puccini's *Madame Butterfly*; musicals — *The Sound of Music, West Side Story, Phantom of the Opera*.]
- *Hallelujah Handel!* combines historical fact with a child-centered fictional drama. As they listen, ask students to consider how they might tell the story in a different form: a journal of impressions, a historical research project, a fictional diary or an illustrated book.

Scene 1: Meeting Handel and Thomas

LENGTH OF SCENE: 13:05 TAPE STARTING POINT: SIDE 1/0:00 CD TRACKS 1–5

BEGINS: *"Rain, rain, rain!"*

ENDS: *"I played my music for a better audience: for the orphans."*

The Story

Handel accompanies Katarina to his last performance of *Messiah*, just two weeks before his death in 1759. They reminisce about their meeting nine years earlier at an exotic English party given by the Duchess of Howland. We are transferred back to that party. There, they meet the famous "centerpiece girl" and Thomas, a boy who sings but does not speak. Thomas collapses and his keeper runs off, so Katarina kindly takes the boy home. After hearing him sing to a choir of spirit children, she takes him to Vauxhall Gardens to find Handel. The composer gleefully recounts stories about an angry tenor and the Fireworks disaster.

The Music

- Sarabande, Harpsichord Suite in D Minor
- Hornpipe, Water Music, Suite No. 2 in D Major
- Andante, Harp Concerto, Op. 4, No. 6, Mvt 1
- "Give Me My Freedom" ("Lascia ch'io pianga"), *Rinaldo*
- Andante, Flute Sonata No. 5 in F Major, Mvt 1
- "Evening Stillness" ("Süsse Stille"), Nine German Arias
- Réjouissance, Music for the Royal Fireworks, Mvt 4
- Overture, Music for the Royal Fireworks, Mvt 1

Background Information

Quotable Handel

Handel was known as a marvelous character, larger-than-life in size, humor, energy, talent and heart. His presence dominated London during the early 1700s, as did Beethoven in Vienna a century later.

Born in Germany, Handel traveled extensively throughout Europe before settling in London in 1712. Consequently, his English bristled with Italian, German and French expressions. Some say he was like the man "who gave up his first tongue without taking the precaution of learning another"! In his day, people teased the composer by misquoting his lovely song, "I Come, My Queen, to Chaste Delights" as "I Comb My Queen to Chase the Lice!" Handel chuckled and cheerfully retorted: "Someday I sprechen the English besserer than you!"

Georgian England and the "Centerpiece Girl"

When Queen Anne failed to produce an heir, Germany's Elector of Hanover was crowned King George I of England. So began an era of unimaginable wealth and appalling poverty.

For those born to money, it was a wondrous time. Property passed undivided to the first son, the Industrial Revolution had not yet defaced the landscape and the beauty of Georgian architecture was unsurpassed.

In the countryside, "lighting the night" became the sign of true wealth. No image better captures the contrast between rich and poor than the manor house on the hill ablaze with flaming torches and surrounded by darkened farm villages where the common people slept before taking up their chores well before dawn.

In the cities, the great houses resembled sparkling jewel boxes, alive with light and music. London buzzed with extravagant teas, balls and charities. Liveried carriages trotted along tree-lined boulevards and silver-gloved servants delivered engraved invitations on silver trays.

During the 1750s, London was captivated by "the centerpiece girl," a beautiful eight-year-old who could quote poetry on demand. Artfully posed on the polished dining table, she would "delight the eye and ravish the ear" of astonished guests.

The Great Fireworks Disaster

To this day, London is famous for its parks of tree-lined meadows and sparkling ponds right in the center of a city. In its world-renowned Vauxhall Gardens, shining carriages discharged elegant passengers, musicians, writers, artists and visitors from Britain's far-reaching empire to promenade beneath trees strung with Chinese lanterns. Lovers embraced in alcoves decorated by Hogarth while connoisseurs sipped the newly popular imported drinks of tea and coffee. Concerts were held in fabulous outdoor stage sets.

Handel's Music for the Royal Fireworks was first heard in Vauxhall Gardens. Written to commemorate the 1748 Peace of Aix-la-Chapelle, this suite included the famous Réjouissance you hear on this recording. Even the rehearsal drew 12,000 people, causing a three-hour traffic jam on London Bridge. The climax of the event was a magnificent fireworks display to be launched from a theatrical set, which had taken six months to build. When a flashpot tipped over, the pavilion burned to the ground and the enraged designer "drew his sword on the Comptroller of his Majesty's Fireworks."

Discussion and Activities

Casting and Accents

Young listeners love imitating the "maah-ve-lous" motor-mouth fictitious Duchess. She is a true upper-class twit who never thinks a thought silently or takes other people's sensitivities into consideration. Nevertheless, we can never get angry at her, for she is truly and innocently silly. Children are great mimics who can develop their ear for other languages through imitation. This little improvisation is a good way to encourage students to play creatively with an accent without mocking it. Ask students to:

- Gossip about a schoolyard event, imitating the Duchess's highly modulated voice, plunging up and down the scale.
- Choose other accents to improvise other situations. For example, use a southern drawl from a cattle round-up or an Australian accent to give directions home.

- Guess what language is fast becoming the international language. [Answer: English.]
- Name other prominent languages from the past. [Answers: Latin in the Roman Empire and Medieval monasteries, French as the language of diplomacy in the 19th century.]

- Write a character description of someone in a book. Pretend you are a casting director for a movie. (It is surprising how children effectively portray character using this technique!)
- Design an advertisement for the Help Wanted section of a theater magazine. Aim for compression in your writing as if you are only allowed a fixed number of words.

Creative Writing: Point of View, Dialogue and Monologue

Like *Vivaldi's Ring of Mystery*, this recording alternates monologue looking backward (e.g., Older Katarina's descriptions before Thomas's songs on Tracks 3 and 4) with dialogue in real time (e.g., at the ball). Explore these literary choices in Scene 1 as follows.

- What is a monologue? [Answer: a single voice speaking.] Dialogue? [Answer: two or more speakers.]
- Write a paragraph about a personal experience in both forms. Or take a story you have already written and change its style.
- Choose some music and read your paragraph over it. Which technique is more responsive to the music, dialogue or monologue?
- Construct a chart like the one here to summarize the differences between the two forms:

DIALOGUE	MONOLOGUE
• Uses shorter sentences • Is written in the present • Humor is quick, direct • Uses questions and answers • Conveys ideas, instructions • Music moves into background for general mood	• Uses longer sentences • Often written in the past • Humor is more "literary" • Uses prose • Conveys descriptions, feelings • Music in foreground, tied closely to words

Sound Effects

Sound effects are powerful tools for creating a sense of location. *Vivaldi's Ring of Mystery* used seagulls, storms and the sounds of gondolas to bring alive the canals of Venice. Ask your class:

- Can you find the eight sound effects used in the opening scene? [Answer: horses' hooves, snorts, carriage wheels, outside ambience, inside ambiance, rain, thunder and wind.]
- Think about your own world. Describe its soundscape. Plan a class outing to collect sound effects using an inexpensive tape recorder. Notice how difficult it is to get "pure" sound effects — thunder without rain, birds without traffic noises. Talk about your discoveries and problems. Can your friends guess what you have recorded? This is a wonderful exercise in listening!

Living in the Past: An Army of Servants

- Show a picture of a Georgian manor house and have your class compile a list of jobs necessary to maintain it. Either write a list or mime actions for the rest of the class to guess. Here are some examples:
  - For her Ladyship: seamstresses, lady's maids and hairdressers
  - For his Lordship: wig makers, menservants and secretaries
  - For the children: wet nurses, governesses and tutors
  - For the kitchens: head cooks, sauce makers, fire tenders, scullery maids
  - For the dining room: butlers and servers
  - For the salon: entertainers, musicians and singers
  - For the bedrooms: housekeepers, housemaids and fire-lighters
  - For outside: groundskeepers, gardeners for fresh flowers and vegetables
  - For stables: horse trainers, stable hands and footmen
  - For country estates: gamekeepers, estate agents, candle makers, cask builders...

  The list goes on!

Body Language and Courtly Games from the Past

An 18th-century visitor to your class would find our body movements, voice modulation and facial expressions very still and inexpressive. People then used extravagant gestures and highly declamative voices. Explore with you students typical positions or gestures of today:

- Show these expressions without words: "I don't know!" "Sure, sure!" "Great play!" Find other examples of body language used today.
- Divide your class into small groups and have them choose a well-known story, poem, picture book or even television show. Have each group design a "tableau" and hold it while the rest of the class guesses the scene. Making tableaux (from the French word for "pictures") used to be a popular parlor game. Young men and women would think of a literary work or famous painting. Then they would costume and pose themselves to resemble the work, and the guests would guess the artistic source or reference.

Exploring the Music

Traveling around Europe as a young man, Handel eagerly absorbed musical ideas from every country. This section explores the Sarabande and the Hornpipe. Both relate to the "pomp" rather than the "piety" of the Baroque era.

Two Sarabandes

One teacher described this effective way of opening a concert: Students paraded into the auditorium in pairs, holding candles and dancing the sarabande as described below. They then sung Thomas's heart-breaking aria, "Give Me My Freedom" from *Rinaldo*.

Two Sarabandes

Sarabande in D Minor

Give Me My Freedom
(or write your own words)

Sarabande in D Minor

The Sarabande in D Minor — A Dance

Ask students:

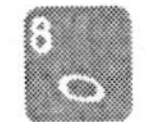

- Can anyone play the opening Sarabande on the piano?
- The sarabande is a stately Spanish dance walk. How many beats does it have? [Answer: three.]
- How would you describe the rhythm? [Answer: halting, with beats (1) medium, (2) long, (3) short.]
- Dance-walk this piece as follows:

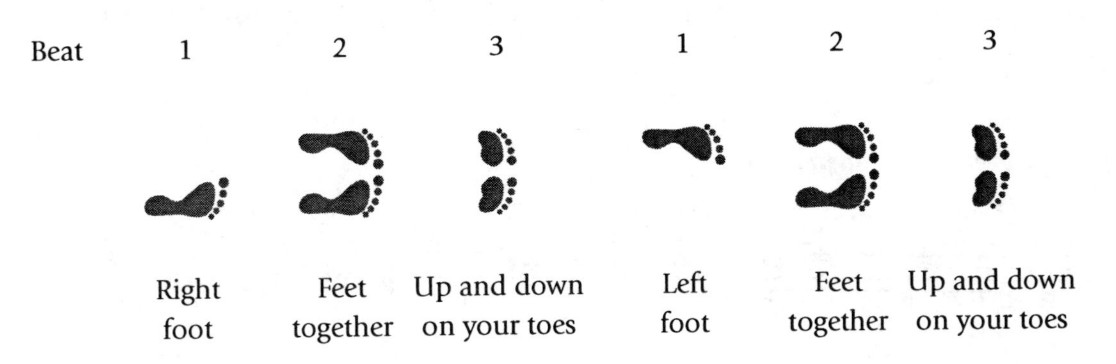

- As a variation, dance the sarabande, in a square by leading first with your right foot to step forward and to the right; then step backwards with the left foot and then to the left to complete the box.

"Give Me My Freedom" — A Song Sarabande

Ask students to:

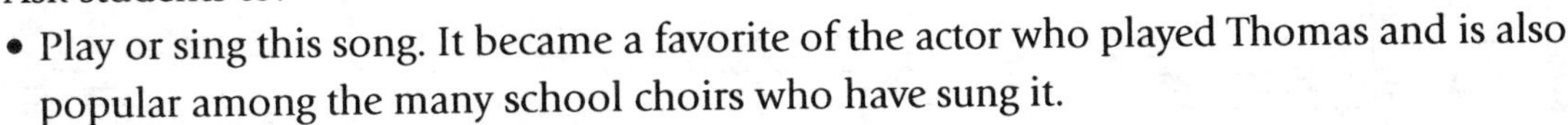

- Play or sing this song. It became a favorite of the actor who played Thomas and is also popular among the many school choirs who have sung it.

- Write your own lyrics and sing them.

- Talk about form da capa form (ABA form). Raise your hand when you hear the theme return.

- This aria is usually sung in Italian. How do opera companies today indicate the English words? [Answer: surtitles, programs with translations.]

- Talk about special effects used at concerts and in theater productions today.

Baroque opera directors also used elaborate stagecraft to make the words come alive. According to records, some productions highlighted "Give Me My Freedom" (Lascia) by releasing real birds into the audience.

Two Hornpipes

Hornpipe in D — Instrumental

Handel excelled at courtly music such as this Hornpipe from the Water Music and the Réjouissance from the Fireworks Music.

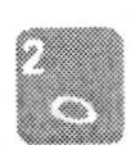

- Enjoy playing the Hornpipe in D as written here for two recorders.
- Add some percussion or glockenspiels to create a sense of majesty.

Réjouissance — Instrumental and Sung Round

Handel sometimes referred to the Fireworks Music as his "big bow-wow" piece. Because King George insisted on "martial instruments and less fiddles," Réjouissance is scored for 9 trumpets, 9 horns, 24 oboes, 12 bassoons, 3 kettle-drums and some strings. Even by today's standards, this is a huge brass section.

- Listen to the recording again and make a chart of its structure in terms of sonority. Let the letter A represent the main theme. [Answer: A brass, A strings, B brass, B strings, A brass, A strings.]

- Réjouissance can be sung as a lively round with only the last few notes altered. Children as young as five enjoy this arrangement. Expand it into a round, adding subsequent voices up to 10 parts!

Hornpipe in D — Instrumental

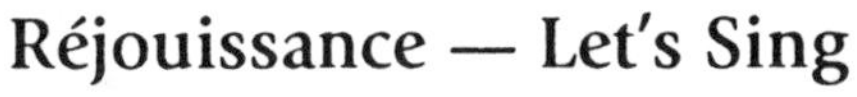

arr. S.H.

Scene 2: The Foundling Hospital

LENGTH OF SCENE: 11:00 TAPE STARTING POINT: SIDE 1/13:05 CD TRACKS 6–10

BEGINS: *"For the orphans: Ach, there are so many of them."*

ENDS: *"Tomorrow then, we meet at the opera!"*

The Story

Handel explains the plight of London's orphans and his efforts to help them. Handel, Katarina and Thomas visit the Foundling Hospital. The choir sings and the music master tells them what he knows about Thomas. Thomas runs off and is found singing by the graveyard. As Handel battles with Madame Cuzzoni at a rehearsal, Thomas laughingly imitates her vocal flourishes. Handel shows the paintings in his harpsichord and playfully explains how musicians are "performing monkeys."

The Music

- Largo, Concerto Grosso, Op. 6, No. 4, Mvt 2
- "See the Conqu'ring Hero Comes," *Judas Maccabaeus*
- "For unto Us a Child Is Born," *Messiah*
- "Golden Sunlight" ("Verdi prati"), *Alcina*
- "Far from Tempest" ("Da tempeste"), *Julius Caesar*
- Chaconne, Harpsichord Suite in G Major

Background Information

An Orphan's Life in the Foundling Hospital

London's Foundling Hospital held the key to *Messiah's* final success in 1750. Venice already boasted four such orphanages, including Vivaldi's Pietà. Created by Thomas Coram "for the Maintenance of Exposed and Deserted Young Children," the Foundling Hospital enlisted the support of artists such as the painter Hogarth. Today, people from all over the world can trace their origin back to the orphanage records, and there is a small lane near the hospital named Handel Street.

What was life like in these orphanages? Babies were accepted by lottery, their mothers drawing colored balls from a sack. If accepted and healthy, the infants were sent into the country for three years with a wet nurse. At three years old, the toddlers returned to the hospital. Children were taught to read but not write, so as to ensure they took only "service" jobs. Boys were trained to become sailors, making fish nets and rope. Girls were taught to become maids, learning to spin and sew. Only blind children were taught music in order to earn money.

On Sundays, the children were dressed in costumes designed by Hogarth to be viewed by "Persons of Quality and Distinction." The guests were treated to Handel's music while viewing works donated by England's best artists. Eventually, a curfew of 7:00 p.m. had to be enforced so the children could get enough sleep for their 5:00 a.m. wake-up. The overall attitude to orphans is best summed up in this notice:

VISITORS ARE REQUESTED TO TAKE NO FAMILIAR NOTICE OF CHILDREN,
LEST IT ENCOURAGE THEM TO FORGET THE LOWNESS OF THEIR STATION

- Read this Girls' Prayer to your class:

Make me dutiful and obedient to my benefactors, and charitable to my enemies.
Make me temperate and chaste, meek and patient, true in all my dealings and content and industrious in my station.

Art and Architecture in the Eighteenth Century

How did England look during Handel's time? Any library will have books of illustrations by English artists such as Hogarth, Gainsborough and Reynolds, as well as by Canaletto, who painted marvelous canvasses of the Thames River. Admire the architecture of Christopher Wren, revel in the Baroque ornamentation of St. Paul's Cathedral and imagine wandering around the elegant oval of Bath's Royal Crescent. As you browse, imagine sitting in Chippendale chairs beside your Adam's fireplace, looking out at your garden designed by Capability Brown.

Discussion and Activities

Why Is Thomas Silent?

A child who does not speak holds enormous pathos and, strangely, power. Ask your class:

- Can you think of other examples of mute characters in fiction or real life? [The movies *House of Cards, Amazing Grace and Chuck*; the musical *Tommy*; books about Helen Keller and *The Lottery Rose*.]
- Can you think of reasons for a child to remain silent? [Suggestions: It feels safer to be silent; the child is enveloped in mute misery, or waiting for something.]
- Write a short story based on a mute character.
- Discuss why Thomas continues to sing even while he does not talk. Suggestions:

  - Singing feels safer than talking because it is distancing and does not involve dialogue.
  - He remembers his mother singing to him as a baby and wants to get closer to her.
  - He needs to express his inner feelings.
  - He is forced by his Keeper to earn money.

Thomas's Story

This scene gives many clues to Thomas's past.

- Ask your students to recount all they know about his past:

  - His mother died when he was young, but he remembers her singing to him. Where?
  - He drifted into the slums of London, choosing to sing but not to speak. Why?
  - He spent some time in the Foundling Hospital, but was sent away. Why?
  - He was sent to Bedlam Hospital, but was bought by a showman. Why?
  - While he was singing at a party, he collapsed. Why?
  - His keeper ran off. Why?
  - He retreated into a dream life, speaking to his mother through song. Why? How often?

- Many children enjoy orphan stories. Name as many orphan stories as you can (e.g., *Anne of Green Gables, Annie, Oliver Twist*).
- How is Thomas's character different than these children?

Monkeys in the Harpsichord

No, Handel did not actually have monkeys living in his harpsichord! They were painted inside the lid. Baroque art was often whimsical, full of angels, cupids and musicians.

- Copy and color this wonderful title page from one of Handel's operas.
- Make title pages for your favorite books using different styles, including this ornate Baroque one.

Exploring the Music

"See the Conqu'ring Hero Comes"

This wonderful song is often played by junior and high school bands. Young people love its steady march time, its satisfying ABA form and infectious rhythm. "See the Conqu'ring Hero Comes" is from *Judas Maccabaeus*, the oratorio that also gave us "O Lovely Peace."

- Play "See the Conqu'ring Hero Comes" on recorders in one or two parts. The top line is more complicated, but the bottom is easy enough for beginners.

- Sing this piece in one or two parts. Choirs who have difficulty with the high G's may prefer to play it in D major.

"For unto Us a Child Is Born"

No one who has sung this chorus from *Messiah* can ever forget the experience.

- Have your class sing along with the choir (at least until they break down in giggles), or join a full rendition from a recording of *Messiah* highlights.

Accented Beats in Messiah

Handel's peculiar inflection of the English language can be found throughout *Messiah*.

- Write these phrases on the board as Handel's music accented them (in capital letters) "FOR unto us a Child is born" "He WAS despised" "He SHALL feed His flock" "HAL-lelujah"

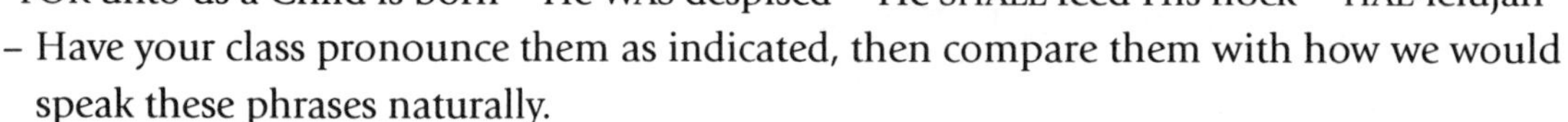

  - Have your class pronounce them as indicated, then compare them with how we would speak these phrases naturally.

Self-borrowings in Messiah

Handel "borrowed" extensively from himself and others. *Messiah* has five instances of self-borrowing. The most famous, "For unto Us", first appeared as a playful Italian duet between two sopranos. This might account for its odd English accents and bouncing beat in an otherwise religious work. While the debate will never be definitively resolved, it can be said that "whatever Handel borrowed, he returned with interest!"

- Is this an example of plagiarism? [Answer: No, you cannot plagiarize yourself.]

"Golden Sunlight" ("Verdi Prati"), Alcina

This aria from *Alcina* is usually sung by a baritone, but is hauntingly beautiful when sung in a child's voice. The opera's plot concerns a sorceress who lives on an enchanted island and turns her lovers into animals or inanimate objects before she can destroy them with her passion. Have your students:

- Sing along with these words: "Golden sunlight, gentle breezes; Waft your blessings in my heart."

- Draw this touching scene of Thomas balancing on the wall or by his mother's grave.

See the Conqu'ring Hero Comes

Scene 3: Opera and Oratorio

LENGTH OF SCENE: 13:30 TAPE STARTING POINT: SIDE 2/0:00 CD TRACKS 11–16

BEGINS: *Orchestral Music: Arrival of the Queen of Sheba*

ENDS: *"Going, going... gone!"*

The Story

Katarina and Thomas attend a performance of the opera *Julius Caesar.* Is Thomas hearing his mother's voice in the soprano's love song? While visiting an English pub, Handel tells the story of his Water Music. The men sing a rousing soldier's song. In the carriage on the way home, Katarina hears an imaginary choir of lost children. Katarina and Thomas visit Handel at his home where he demonstrates word-painting in *Messiah*.

The Music

- Arrival of the Queen of Sheba, *Solomon*
- Sinfonia, *Julius Caesar*
- "Set Your Arms to the Battle" ("In tal modi"), *Julius Caesar*
- Sinfonia to "V'adoro," *Julius Caesar*
- "I Love You, My Treasure" ("V'adoro"), *Julius Caesar*
- Bourrée, Music for the Royal Fireworks, Mvt 2
- Air, Water Music Suite No. 1 in F Major
- "Stand Round My Brave Boys," Song for Gentlemen Volunteers
- "O Lovely Peace," *Judas Maccabaeus*
- "The Harmonious Blacksmith," Harpsichord Suite in E Major
- Pastoral Symphony, *Messiah*
- "There Were Shepherds," *Messiah*
- "Glory to God," *Messiah*

Background Information

Life at the Opera

Opera was considered essential to an aristocrat's life. Those who did not like music could escape to curtained boxes and adjoining card rooms. Londoners could even claim a full ticket refund if they left before the first note!

For composers, the opera was a difficult place to gain success. Eighteenth-century London was particularly competitive. Audiences and patrons set singer against singer, composer against composer, theater against theater, and company against company.

By 1735, Handel was locked in mortal battle with an opposing opera company, the Opera of the Nobility. This group ousted Handel from his favorite Haymarket Theatre, stole his singers and emptied his opera halls. As a result, he suffered a stroke from which he miraculously recovered in the baths of Aix-la-Chapelle.

Madame Cuzzoni Meets Her Match

Handel's troubles did not end with opposing opera companies and frivolous audiences. In the 1730s, London rocked with stories of his battles with Italian singers. Today's hockey fights pale by comparison with life in an 18th-century opera hall! Gossip magazines of the day described the "most diverting scenes of two sopranos on stage, locked in a mortal combat, scratching faces and pulling wigs." Divas often insisted on including their favorite arias from other composers in Handel's operas!

In one famous incident, Handel actually picked up the headstrong Madame Cuzzoni and hung her over the balcony. During another performance, he was so enraged by her attempts to gain applause by delaying the final note that he declared: "Madame, you are welcome home!"

The Castrati Question

We will never hear Handel's operas as he heard them because so many roles were given to the eunuch superstars. According to an Italian practice, young boy sopranos were castrated to preserve their high voices. Castrati trained for years to produce notes and trills up to one minute long. Combining the range of a woman with the strength of a man, their voices carried to the very back of the hall without benefit of modern microphones hidden in wigs.

Today, we can only imagine the sound. In fact, the movie *Farinelli* tried to recreate a castrato voice by digitally combining a female soprano with a male counter-tenor. A recording is available of the last castrato, who died in 1903.

Calling All Set Designers

Handel's theaters dazzled audiences with spectacular theatrical effects including live birds and animals, choreographed dancing and fully staged battles. In the absence of revolving stages, designers created remarkable effects with simple panels painted in dramatically receding perspectives. Powered by wooden winches, these "flats" slid in grooves angled toward the back of the theater. Partially closed, they created the optical illusion of immense depth; fully closed, they made a shallow stage behind which moons and chariots could be lowered into position. Because the curtain never fell between acts, scene changes were executed in full view of the audience.

London's opera halls were also marvels in lighting. Candles flickered in footlights in front of the stage. Other candles affixed to the back of flats became hidden sources of light for the painted scenes behind them. Actors wore clothing stitched with silver and gold to reflect the warm lighting. Many used white grease paint and gloves to emphasize Baroque hand movements and expressive faces.

Handel's Great Coup: Water Music

When George of Hanover came to the English throne, Handel inherited a difficult situation. As a young man, Handel had abandoned this very monarch in order to travel to Italy and England. A friend suggested that he gain favor with the new king by writing some music for a royal outing on the Thames. Handel rented a barge, filled it with 50 musicians and serenaded the king with his Water Music. The king was delighted. Today, the Air from his Suite No. 1 and the Hornpipe from Suite No. 2 are known almost as well as *Messiah*.

Countless books have been written on the subject of Handel's *Messiah*. It is a work that seems to reach beyond 18th-century London, Handel and even classical music itself, right into our hearts today.

Composition

By 1741, Handel's problems with opera had reached a crisis point. His fights with the Opera of the Nobility, a cold winter that kept patrons at home near their warm fires, the war between England and Spain, and the attacks by middle-class Puritans on all "frivolous entertainments" took their toll on his health and purse. With opera in decline, Handel turned to producing oratorios instead.

The following chart lists the differences between oratorio and opera.

OPERA	ORATORIO
• secular, often classical, subjects • words in frequently in Italian or German • performed in theaters • used staging effects for drama • Handel wrote 42 • examples in this recording: *Julius Caesar, Rinaldo, Alcina*	• religious subjects • words in English • performed in churches, halls • used choruses for drama • Handel wrote 19 • examples in this recording: *Judas Maccabaeus, Alexander's Feast, Samson, Solomon, Messiah*

Handel began composing *Messiah* on August 21, 1741, one month after the death of Vivaldi. Three weeks later, on September 14, he laid down his pen, having completed one of music's masterpieces. He wrote in a white heat: 275 pages of flying ink and violent smudges. Now 56 years old, he was seized by a religious fervor that would not let him sleep or eat for days. He wept, howled and (according to later sources) declared:

> *Whether I was in my body or out of my body as I wrote it, I know not. I did think I did see all Heaven before me and the great God Himself.*

This frantic activity may be partially explained by Handel's manic depression.

Content and Style

We generally hear *Messiah* around Christmas, but it was actually written for Easter. The libretto (script) was written by Charles Jennens and is divided into three parts. Broadly speaking, they cover Christ's birth, death and resurrection.

Part of *Messiah's* success derives from its adaptability to almost any musical group. Although well over three hours long, it requires only four vocal soloists, a harpsichordist, some strings, two trumpets and a kettledrum (Handel later added two oboes). Furthermore, if one soloist has difficulty with an aria, someone else can sing it. Unlike opera, *Messiah* has no fixed plot that would tie an aria to a specific vocalist.

First Performance

What a wonderful irony that *Messiah*, the world's great religious piece, was born in a pub! In 1742, Handel set out for Dublin with only a sheaf of musical parts, a servant, a secretary and Madame Cibber, his favorite mezzo-soprano. To avoid the notoriously bad Welsh roads, the group traveled north in England before sailing to Ireland. When a storm delayed their crossing, Handel took the opportunity to rehearse some Messiah parts at the Golden Falcon pub in Chester.

The famous English diarist Charles Burney (1726–1814) was then 16 years old and wrote an account of this rehearsal by local amateurs. When a man named Janson had difficulty with his notes, Handel said irritably, "I thought you said you sung at sight." Replied Janson, "Yes sir, but not at first sight!"

Messiah's premiere in Dublin on April 13, 1742, was a great success. To make room for a larger audience, ladies were asked to remove the hoops from their skirts and gentlemen to leave their swords at home. He also conducted several benefit concerts for the wonderfully named "Decayed Musicians and their Families."

Unfortunately, *Messiah* took much longer to be accepted in London. After only five performances in the 1740s, it was retired. Handel had to wait for the 1750 association with the Foundling Hospital until his masterpiece found its place in history.

Messiah Monster Concerts

Messiah's popularity continued to skyrocket after 1750. Share the following facts with your students:

- In 1784, 25 years after Handel's death, 500 performers packed Westminster Abbey to sing *Messiah*. Three years later, their numbers rose to 806.
- In 1791 (the year of Mozart's *The Magic Flute*), so many performers filled Westminster that the audience overflowed all the way up to Trafalgar Square. Families brought their own music to sing along with a concert blocks away!
- Workers from the industrial mills of Victorian England walked miles to rehearse. Because of *Messiah*, music literacy soared.
- London's Crystal Palace became the venue of monster concerts. An 1882 production featured 4,500 performers, enough to fill a large symphony hall with musicians *only*. Even today's rock concerts in massive sports arenas seldom match *Messiah's* record audience of 87,869 people.

Discussion and Activities

Visual Arts: Julius Caesar

The story of Julius Caesar and Cleopatra has fascinated storytellers from Shakespeare to Hollywood. Here are some activities to do with your class on this wonderful romance.

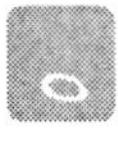

- Tell the story of how a tough Roman soldier won the heart of the exotic Queen of Egypt and briefly joined two empires. What happened to Julius Caesar? [Answer: He was killed by his best friend Brutus.] What happened to Cleopatra? [Answer: She took her life by letting a poison asp bite her.]

- Borrow or rent the video *Cleopatra*. It vividly brings to life the lush opulence Handel was trying to capture in his opera. Older classes will enjoy the entire four-hour epic. Younger children might watch the excerpts showing Cleopatra's famed entrance into Rome and aboard her pleasure boat.
- Have your class listen again to this excerpt from *Hallelujah Handel!* while they draw Cleopatra's magic garden or the battle scene.

Messiah

Composing *Messiah* in just three weeks was not only a mental feat, but a physical one as well.

- Give your class an appreciation of how difficult it is to write musical notation with the following short exercise.
  - Bring in ink and nib pens or even have the children collect bird quills.
  - Stain some paper with coffee, to give feel of parchment
  - Draw several five-line staves in ink. Add clefs and some notes.
  - Run your hand across the ink. Does it smear?
  - Sprinkle some talcum powder on it. Does that help dry and fix the ink?
- Use your art materials to paint a scene or mural from *Messiah*, such as the shepherds out in the starlit fields or down in the village with their bagpipes.

Character Development

A good story needs character development.

- Ask your students to list clues that Thomas is beginning to reach out and that his mood is improving, such as:
  - He playfully imitates Madame Cuzzoni in rehearsal.
  - He smiles at the monkeys in Handel's harpsichord.
  - He almost reaches out for his mother at the opera.
  - He joins Katarina in practicing *Messiah*.

Exploring the Music

Julius Caesar

How sad that of the 42 operas Handel wrote, we know only a few arias, including the famous "Largo" from *Xerxes*, "Where'ere You Walk" from *Semele* and the five arias on this recording. Even less familiar is his wonderful orchestral music, such as this Battle Sinfonia from *Julius Caesar* and the Arrival of the Queen of Sheba from *Solomon*. They are certainly equal in excitement to his Fireworks or Water Music.

Especially miraculous is the orchestral introduction to the song "I Love You, My Treasure" ("V'adoro"). Handel asks for two entire orchestras, one in the pit and one on stage. The musical lines twine sensuously around each other while the harp adds a glowing, other-worldly effect.

The following aria by Cleopatra is one of Baroque music's greatest treasures. For advanced classes, bring in a recording of the entire aria (on most Baroque highlight soprano albums). Then have your class:

- Study the ABA form of the da capa aria. Show the return of the opening theme by conducting the last statement.
- Describe how Handel embellishes the last cadence.
- Sing this wonderful aria in a school concert.
- Listen to more of *Julius Caesar.* ("Set Your Arms to the Battle," "I Shall Weep" and "Far from the Tempest" are also on this recording.)

Four Great Pastorales

Some of the best-loved pieces in classical music describe nature. Often written in the "pastoral key" of F major and sharing a relaxed rhythm, these timeless pieces soothe our hurried souls. Movements from Handel's Water Music, Vivaldi's "The Four Seasons," Bach's Orchestral Suites and Beethoven's "Shepherd's Theme" (Symphony No. 6) can refresh us with their simple melodies.

Air from the Water Music

The Air is rich in classroom possibility. Let your class enjoy it as below:

- *Instruments:* Play this melody on one or two recorders. Even the youngest child can manage the simple glockenspiel part. The first eight bars are most familiar, and older students might try playing the entire piece as written here.
- *Singing:* Write some lyrics to this simple melody and sing it (e.g., "Sailing on the sea/ ocean waves; I can see the fish/at play").
- *Dance:* Find a movement or pantomime to interpret this music. Use streamers.
- *Spoken Word:* Write a poem and read it over the music.
- *Art:* Draw whatever scene this music suggests to you.

"O Lovely Peace," Judas Maccabaeus

Surely Handel wrote no more lovely melody than this chorus from *Judas Maccabaeus*. It is very much like Beethoven's "Shepherd's Theme" (Symphony No. 6), included on page 27 so you can compare the two.

- Sing the two songs separately.
- Sing the two melodies on top of each other. You will find two instances when you have to change a note to assist the harmonies.

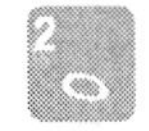

- Play "O Lovely Peace" on recorders. Use the single line written here, or add a second parallel voice a third below the melody. Glockenspiels can be added by ear and need only three notes: D, A and G.

Air from the Water Music

Beethoven's Shepherd's Theme

Arr. Susan Hammond

O Lovely Peace

Arr. Susan Hammond

The "Pifa" from Messiah

Messiah's Pastoral Symphony is sometimes called the "Pifa" because it is like the music played by Italian bagpipes. In form, it is an Italian "sicilienne."

- Ask students to describe its rhythm. [Answer: gently rocking in 12/8 time.]

"He Shall Feed His Flock" from Messiah

Look at these two fragments below and describe their similarities:

- Both pieces are harmonically simple and can be played over a repeated "drone note."
- Both move by step, one in an ascending direction, the other in a descending direction.
- Both are in 12/8 time and are almost exact inversions of each other.

He Shall Feed His Flock

Investigating Further into Handel's Messiah

Notice the simplicity of Katarina's first solo, "There Were Shepherds Abiding in the Fields." Called a recitative, it features a single vocal line with simple chords on the harpsichord and sometimes a cello. The melody is not as developed as in an aria. Baroque composers used recitatives to tell a story; arias and choruses then reflected on what was happening.

"Glory to God" is the first place in *Messiah* where Handel uses trumpets. He originally asked that they be played offstage, "from far off and soft," to reflect the angels disappearing during the last "Glory to God."

Ask your class:

- How does the music capture the images in the text? [Answer: Fluttering 16th notes imitate angel wings, and the whispered ascent of violin notes eloquently describes their departure into heaven.]
- Compare Younger Katarina's voice with that of Thomas. The actor who sang her part is 16 years old. By putting into words exactly what you hear, you can improve your own performance in terms of interpretation and experimentation with different tone-qualities.
- What words are sung when the boy soprano takes over? [Answer: "Fear not, for behold."]
- What is the difference between the female and male voices? [Answer: The boy's voice is pure, sometimes less exactly placed than the girl's.]

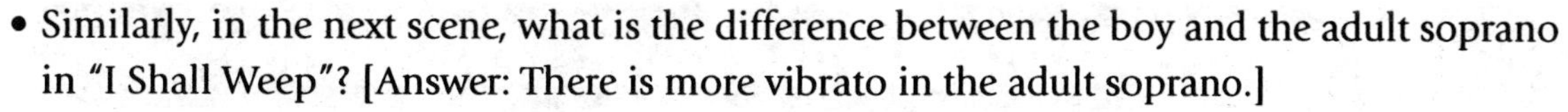

- Similarly, in the next scene, what is the difference between the boy and the adult soprano in "I Shall Weep"? [Answer: There is more vibrato in the adult soprano.]

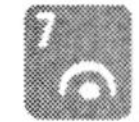

- Listen again to the "Glory to God" scene and then progress to a full recording of excerpts. Play it anywhere, anytime!

The Harmonious Blacksmith

This set of variations from the Suite in E Major is often played by young pianists. Handel did not actually name it "The Harmonious Blacksmith," but many hear the ringing of the anvil in its rhythm.

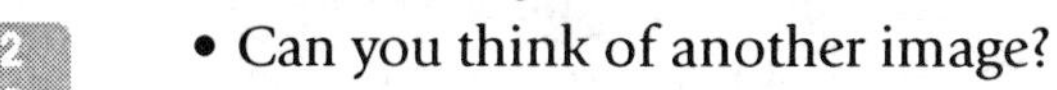

- Can you think of another image?
- Play it by ear, or sing along.
- Make up your own lyrics (e.g., "Do you like to run with the wind, Oh, do you want to run with me?")

Scene 4: Angels in the Opera House, Conclusion

LENGTH OF SCENE: 10:33 TAPE STARTING POINT: SIDE 2/13:30 CD TRACKS 17–20

BEGINS: *"Open up, I know you've got him in there!"*

ENDS: *Conclusion: "I hear the final chord."*

The Story

The Keeper kidnaps Thomas from Handel's house. Handel and Katarina search London's back streets for the boy. They find him standing alone by a single candle on the opera house stage, singing to his spirit mother. Handel reassures Thomas of the healing power of music. We prepare for the benefit concert. The Duchess joins the audience entering the Foundling Hospital for the performance. During the singing of "He Shall Feed His Flock," Thomas hears the voice of his mother. She sings lovingly to him, then bids him goodbye. Thomas answers her with his first spoken words, "Goodbye, Mother." The Hallelujah Chorus ends the concert. In the epilogue, Katarina and Handel are back in the carriage, as in the prologue in Scene 1. Nine years have passed since the benefit concert. They are returning from Handel's very last performance of *Messiah*. Katarina reassures him that he will always be remembered.

The Music

- Sinfonia, *Samson*
- "The People That Walked in Darkness," *Messiah*
- "I Shall Weep" ("Piangerò"), *Julius Caesar*
- Andante, Concerto Grosso, Op. 6, No. 8, Mvt 2
- "He Shall Feed His Flock," *Messiah*
- Hallelujah Chorus, *Messiah*
- "I Know That My Redeemer Liveth," *Messiah*

Background Information

Gin Lane and Bedlam Hospital

Handel and Katarina search for Thomas in London's notorious Gin Lane. Hogarth immortalized this street in his famous picture showing parents drinking gin to drown their misery while feeding their children laudanum (a form of morphine) to keep them quiet. Even though stealing so much as a handkerchief was punishable by death, desperate older children terrorized the area as members of the "dark raiders." Eventually, in Victorian England these slums were torn down.

Bedlam Hospital was London's infamous "madhouse," where patients were often chained like animals and psychiatric help was primitive, to say the least.

Handel's Blindness

Writing by candlelight took its toll on both Handel and Bach. In fact, the same English eye surgeon, Dr. John Taylor, operated unsuccessfully on both composers. Bach died of complications in 1750, and Handel was totally blind by 1753. The Countess of Shaftesbury wrote at the time:

> *It drew tears of sorrow to see the great, though unhappy, Handel, dejected, wan and dark, sitting by, not playing on the harpsichord.*

Handel's Death and Burial

On April 6, 1759, Handel attended his last performance of *Messiah*. That night, he took to his bed and died eight days later on April 14 — 17 years and one day after *Messiah's* Good Friday premiere in Dublin.

Handel was buried in Westminster Abbey in a service attended by 3,000 people. A month later, a memorial service was held in the chapel of the Foundling Hospital. Tickets were printed on mourning paper sealed with black wax. The *Whitehall Evening Post* published this eulogy:

> *To melt the soul, to captivate the ear, Angels his melody might deign to hear.*

Three years later, a statue of Handel was erected in the Poet's Corner of Westminster Abbey. Handel is depicted holding the music to "I Know That My Redeemer Liveth," the piece that ends this recording.

Handel's Posthumous Fame — You Will Never Be Forgotten!

We leave Handel troubled over the question: "Katarina, will anyone remember my music when I'm gone?" In reality, the answer came very soon. With Handel's death, London woke up to its loss. Shops filled with souvenirs of the composer: portraits, engravings, shirt pins, brooches and illustrated fans.

Handel never knew how deeply he influenced later composers. Mozart preferred Bach but loved Handel's *Messiah* enough to write the orchestration that is usually used today. He is quoted as saying:

> *Of all of us, Handel knows best how to produce great effects; where he desires to produce it, he crushes like thunder.*

Beethoven died with a volume of Handel's music by his bed. He loved Handel above all other composers, saying:

> *Handel is the greatest composer that ever lived... I would uncover my head and kneel down at his tomb.*

Chronology of Handel's Life

Here is a summary of Handel's life, including a comparison to his great contemporary, Johann Sebastian Bach (see also *Mr. Bach Comes to Call*).

- Handel was born on February 23, 1685, one month before Bach (March 21).
- He was born in Halle, Germany, very near to Bach's birthplace in Eisenach.
- His father was a barber-surgeon. Bach's father was a musician.
- Handel's father wanted his son to become a lawyer. Bach was expected to follow in the music business.
- Handel's father died when he was 12 years old. Bach's father died when Bach was 11.
- Young Handel taught himself to play on a clavichord that his Aunt Anna sneaked into the attic. Bach furtively copied the Midnight Manuscript.
- Handel, like Bach, went to Lübeck to hear Buxtehude and to apply for his job. Both young men left upon realizing that the job involved marrying Buxtehude's daughter.
- At 21, Handel went to Italy for four years of study and performing. At age 25, he became Kapellmeister to the Elector of Hanover, the future George I. Bach remained closer to home.

Continuing Handel's life:

- In 1712, Handel made London his home where *Rinaldo* ("Give Me My Freedom") was a huge success.
- Three years later, to please the recently crowned King George I, Handel wrote his Water Music.
- In 1719, Handel joined the Royal Academy of Music (which is still active in London today). Soon after, he wrote two books of harpsichord suites (including "The Harmonious Blacksmith").
- In 1723, Madame Cuzzoni arrived in London to sing in *Julius Caesar*.
- Four years later, "Zadok the Priest" was played at the coronation of George II. This anthem has been played for every British coronation since.
- *Alcina* ("Golden Sunlight") opened in 1735 and was a great success. Problems with the Opera of the Nobility lead to Handel's stroke, from which he recovered at Aix-la-Chapelle. In 1741, the last performance of a Handel opera was performed. After that, he turned to oratorio.
- The first performance of *Messiah* was held in Dublin in 1742. Five years later, *Judas Maccabaeus* premiered and in 1749, Handel composed the Music for the Royal Fireworks.
- In 1750, the first successful performance of *Messiah* was performed in London to benefit the Foundling Hospital. Four months later, Johann Sebastian Bach died.
- Handel had his first eye operation in 1750, at the age of 65. By 68, he was completely blind.
- On April 14, 1759, George Frideric Handel died at home at 25 Brook Street, London.
- His manuscripts are now held in the British Museum. His tomb is in Westminster Abbey.
- On the 25th anniversary of his death, the first massive *Messiah* concert was performed.

Discussion and Activities

Spirit Voices and a Troubled Child

Today's movies often feature a guardian spirit who watches over a loved one on earth. Sometimes they are angels, sometimes inner voices to a central troubled character. Ask your class:

- Why do you think guardian spirits might be popular today? [Suggestions: We feel out of control of our lives. We are searching for spirituality in a secular age.]
- What are some examples of these movies. [Answers: *Ghost, The Secret Garden* and *Into of the West.*]
- Borrow or rent one of these movies and discuss it in comparison to *Hallelujah Handel!*
- What are the two spirits or supernatural presence that we meet in this recording? [Answer: in Scene 1, a choir of "lost children"; in the same scene, Thomas's real guardian angel, his mother.]
- How does this scene represent a crisis point for Thomas? [Answer: He believes he meets his mother in the opera house and she tells him she can leave because he is safe in the Foundling Hospital.]
- How does Handel try to bring him back to reality? [Answer: He describes how he got over some very dark times, and was restored to health by the power of music. Music is Thomas's fragile hold on reality.]
- Discuss the subtitle "Angels in the Opera House." Is Thomas the angel? Is it his mother?
- Draw the evocative scene of Thomas singing by the light of a single candle in the empty opera house. Questions to consider: Would you prefer realistic or surrealistic sets? Is the mother hovering above her child? Can you weave a title or quotation into the picture (in the stars, smoke from a taper or wrapped around the halo of the candlelight)?

The Final Concert

The final concert draws together all the characters of the story. Ask your students:

- What is the dramatic reason for the reappearance of the Duchess? [Answers: for a burst of energy, for humor and as a reminder that Thomas is still silent.]
- How do the words to "He Shall Feed His Flock" relate to the subplot about Thomas? [Answer: They are words of comfort about people being protected, just like Thomas is in the orphanage.]
- As you listen, what is your mental picture of the chapel scene? Where are Katarina, Thomas, Handel, Thomas's mother and the children's choir?
- Why does Thomas speak at last? [Answer: He knows he is safe.]

Creative Writing: The Epilogue

As mentioned earlier, this story takes place in two time frames: "reminiscing time" (1750) when *Messiah* first swept London, and "real time" (1759). Ask your class about the epilogue:

- What are the two themes that Katarina and Handel reflect upon? [Answers: Handel's immortality, and how music can heal the soul.]
- Handel's last words are, "Ah, bene... Come, blow out the candle... I hear the final chord." For what is this a metaphor? [Answer: his own coming death in just two weeks.]

Bookends — Prologues and Epilogues

Classes familiar with *Beethoven Lives Upstairs* and *Hallelujah Handel!* will see that both stories use a prologue and an epilogue. Ask your students:

- What is the purpose of a prologue? [Answers: to set the scene, a flashforward or flash-back.]
- What is the purpose of an epilogue? [Answer: to let us know what happens after the action is over, to give the moral to the story.]
- What is the time frame of the prologue and epilogue? [Answer: two weeks before Handel dies in 1759.]
- Who are the speakers? [Answer: Older Katarina and Older Handel.]
- How are they different from the "reminiscing time" characters? [Answer: only in their age. Katarina was only 16 when she first met Handel. He was six years younger, too.]
- Add a prologue and/or epilogue to a story you have already written. You will need some linking phrases back into "reminiscing time." For example, "I never knew how that night would change my life" or "Years later, I found this letter."

Can Music Cure?

The healing power of music was realized as early as the Greeks. Music therapists have shown how music can soothe, focus or stimulate people with emotional or intellectual difficulties. Research shows that thought travels along the same neural pathways as music. Music can stimulate the limbic system, which defines our emotions. The brain is generally stimulated by organized sound, one reason why many children like to work with music on. Discuss with your class:

- Think about this statement: While we can shut our eyes, we cannot shut our ears. Is one sense more primitive than the other? More important?
- How do music preferences reflect our personality? What are your favorite singers?
- How was music a source of joy and torment for Thomas? [Answer: Positively, it was a reaching out to the real world, an escape into a gentler world, a powerful memory. Negatively, it was enforced by his cruel keeper.]
- How was music a mixed blessing for Handel? [Answer: He found writing music to be exhilerating; he felt a terrible emptiness when he was ill and could not write; it was the best way he could connect with others; it was a way to reach out for immortality.]

Exploring the Music

Gin Lane

The music playing during Gin Lane is "The People That Walked in Darkness" from *Messiah.*

- How does Handel reflect these words in his music? [Answer: strings in unison, stepping from note to note, in a dark minor key.]

6

"I Shall Weep" ("Piangerò" from *Julius Caesar*)

This aria is sung by Cleopatra in prison as she weeps for her loss of Caesar. It is a hit on virtually every album of soprano excerpts. Listen to "Piangerò" in its entirety.

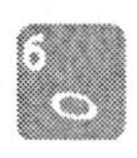

- What instruments does Handel use to create the surreal beauty of the vocal line? [Answer: harp and high flute.]
- What is the difference in timbres between the boy and the female soprano? [Answer: The woman has more vibrato in her singing.]

Two Great Siciliennes: "He Shall Feed His Flock"

Handel appears to love musical forms that begin with the letter "s": the two sarabandes in the first scene, and the two siciliennes here at the end.

"He Shall Feed His Flock" is one of the great siciliennes of all time, a universal lullaby. Refer back to the comparison of this piece with the "Pifa" in the previous scene, and ask:

- What is its time signature? [Answer: 12/8.]
- What instruments are used in the accompaniment? [Answer: strings.]
- Listen for the emotional and harmonic lift when Handel begins the soprano solo four notes higher than the chorus in 12/8 time. Handel uses only simple strings to highlight the voices.

"I Know That My Redeemer Liveth"

This wonderful piece for mezzo-soprano is carved into Handel's statue in Westminster Abbey. In this recording, the voice is replaced by the oboe, because it so closely resembles the human voice. In this glowing moment, script and music come together. Ask your class:

- What instrument underscores Katarina's voice? [Answer: the oboe.]
- What instrument underscores Handel's voice? [Answer: strings.]

The Hallelujah Chorus

If you supplement this recording with only one piece of music, make it the Hallelujah Chorus. Every child deserves to hear this piece at least once during his or her lifetime! It is the source of our title, and is one of the most famous songs in the English language. Part of the power of the Hallelujah Chorus comes from its simple structure. Ask your students:

- How many "Hallelujahs" are in the opening sequence? [Answer: five.]
- What happens next? [Answer: The whole series is then repeated one note higher.]
- How often is the next phrase, "For the Lord God Omnipotent reigneth," repeated? [Answer: twice.]

- Describe the rest of the chorus. [Answer: Handel tosses his themes back and forth in a joyous Baroque fugue, then follows it with a quiet middle section in block chords, before returning to the ringing Hallelujahs.]
- How does he dramatize the ending? [Answer: With a long pause before the last Hallelujah.]
- How is Handel inconsistent with English pronunciation? [Answer: In the first statement alone, he stresses three different syllables: "HAL-lelujah, Halle-LU-jah, Hal-LE-lujah."]

It is traditional for audiences to stand during the entire Hallelujah Chorus. This practice began when King George II unexpectedly stood during up during its singing. Naturally, his subjects could not remain seated while their sovereign stood. We will never know why King George chose to stand. Was he so moved by the music? Did he think the piece was over? Or did he simply have to use the royal chamber pot?

After the Recording

Questions to ask:

- Which scenes do you like best? Are they the lively funny sections, or the sad heart-tugging moments? Who is your favorite character? Which music did you like best?

- Listen to Handel's music during quiet time or other activities. Recommended works include the Water Music, Music for the Royal Fireworks and *Messiah*. Even better, invite some musicians in to play some of his music!
- Pretend you are a newspaper entertainment reporter who has just received *Hallelujah Handel!* Write a review commenting on the script, the quality of the acting, the use of music and the effectiveness of sound effects.

- Be reporters and interview Handel about some of the true stories from the recording: How did he name his Water Music? What happened at the end of the Fireworks Music? How did the music and staging of *Julius Caesar* bring the story alive? Why did Handel threaten to throw the soprano out the window?
- If you were a movie producer, which sections would you emphasize? From whose point of view would you tell the story? What music, sound or lighting effects would you include? Would you use a prologue and epilogue?
- Although Thomas's story is told from Katarina's point of view, discuss other ways this story could have been written. [Suggestions: biographical fiction (third person), diary (first person) or illustrated book.]
- Make a storyboard of the plot. Use different colored inks to represent fictional and true events.
- If your classroom has other Classical Kids recordings, try to name similarities and differences between the composers, their times and the role of the fictional child.
- Show your class movies with similar themes: *House of Cards, Into the West, The Secret Garden, Cleopatra, Farinelli, The Madness of King George.*
- Make a chart of musical excerpts, their instrumentation and tempo/mood. Start at the beginning of Scene 1 and proceeding through to the end. For example:
  - Sarabande, low strings, slow and dark
  - Hornpipe, strings and trumpet, festive and fast
  - Harp Concerto, harp and strings, moderato and polite... etc.
- Make your own Baroque production. Use the songs, dances, sets, and tableaux described here as a starting point.
- Do a research project on England and Handel. Make a comparison with the two other Baroque composers: Bach and Vivaldi.

Classical Kids and the Integrated Curriculum

This chart and the following 10-day Lesson Plan illustrate the themes and skills developed in these Teacher's Notes for *Hallelujah Handel!*

There is also a sample question sheet after the Lesson Plan for those teachers wishing to assess their students' skills and knowledge with a short test.

Core Area	Handel
Time Frame	1685–1759
Geography	England
Social Studies	• Georgian England • Foundling Hospital • Vauxhall Gardens • Gin Lane
Creative Writing	• Prologues and epilogues • Dialogues and monologues • Storyboards • Character • Orphan tales • Humor
Modern Issues	• Mutism • Guardian angels • Music therapy
Other Arts	• Tableaux • Stage sets • Title pages • Architecture • Artists • Gesture and movement • Sound effects • Movies • Class production
Music	• Opera and oratorio • Singing and playing • *Julius Caesar,* da capa arias • *Messiah* and tone painting • Water music, fireworks • Analysis • Biography
Math and science	• Staging machinery

Suggested Lesson Plan

Week One

MONDAY	TUESDAY	WEDNESDAY	THURSDAY	FRIDAY
Side One • Katarina's story (7) • Thomas's story (16) • Silent children and angels (7) • Spirit voices (33)	**Side Two** • How Thomas is better (24) • Final concert (33) **Social History** • Vauxhall Gardens (9) • Georgian England (8, 16) • Life in the Great Houses (7, 11) • Foundling Hospital (15) • Gin Lane (30) • Georgian project (36)	**Drama** • Accents (9–10) • Body language (11) • Tableaux (8) **Dance** • Sarabande (11–13) **Music** • "Give Me My Freedom" (12) • Hornpipe (14) • Round (14)	**Visual Arts** • Set design (21, 24) • Title page (17) • Art and architecture (16) • Monkeys in the harpsichord (17) • Cleopatra's garden (24) • *Messiah* scene (24) • Air (25) • Making scores (24)	**Language Arts** • Point of view (10, 36) • Prologue and epilogue (34) • Dialogue and monologue (10) • Humor (9, 33)

Week Two

MONDAY	TUESDAY	WEDNESDAY	THURSDAY	FRIDAY
Biography • Handel's life and death (31) • Opera life (20) • Chronology (32) • Character (7) • Posthumous fame (31) **Music** • Air on recorder (26)	**Messiah** • Borrowings (18) • Inflection (18, 36) • Premiere (23) • Monster concerts (23) • Tone painting (28) • Hallelujah (35) • "For unto Us" (18) • "Pifa" (6) • "He Shall Feed" (28, 35) • "I Know That My Redeemer" (35)	**Music** • Opera, oratorio, musicals (7, 22) • Castrati and Cuzzoni (21) • *Julius Caesar* (24) • Pastorales (25) • Water Music (22) **Music Analysis** • "The Harmonious Blacksmith" (29) • Mapping sonority (36)	**Music** • "Conqu'ring Hero" (18) • "O Lovely Peace" (25, 27) • Sinfonia, "I Love You" (24) **Other Arts** • Sound effects (10) • Music therapy (34) • Spirit voices, troubled child (33)	**Review and Compare** • Retelling story (36) • Reportage (36) • Movies of similar themes or images: *House of Cards, Into the West, The Secret Garden, Cleopatra, Farinelli, The Madness of King George* (36) • Worksheet (39)

Option for Advanced Classes

MONDAY	TUESDAY	WEDNESDAY	THURSDAY	FRIDAY
• Plan a class production: script, casting, movement, songs, sets, costumes, dance	• Select music and rehearse songs (12, 14, 19, 26, 27)	• Choreograph dances	• Set construction and costumes • Rehearse	• Present concert

Worksheet for Hallelujah Handel!

1. Handel was born in the year of ________.
   He died in __________ at the age of ____.
2. He grew up in ____________, traveled in ______________ and ______________, then settled in the city of ______________, where he lived most of his life.
3. The opening scene is set in a ___________, where Handel is traveling with __________ to a concert in the year _______.
4. Name the four people in this recording who have funny or interesting accents. _______
5. Name as many sound effects as you can remember on the recording. ____________
6. List three funny sayings by Handel. _______
7. What are Thomas's problems? __________
8. What is he doing at the party, and why does he fall over? ______________________
9. Who takes him home to take care of him?
10. Why does the choir break down in giggles when singing "For unto Us"? ___________
11. Why does Thomas tease Madame Cuzzoni?
12. What is the setting of the scene from *Julius Caesar?* ______________________
13. What is Cleopatra singing about? _______
14. Give four clues that Thomas is getting better. ______________________
15. What is the story of the *Messiah* scene? ____
16. Who steals Thomas away? ______________
17. Where do Katarina and Handel find him?
18. What is Thomas doing when they find him?
19. What happens during the final concert?
20. What is your favorite scene? ___________
21. What is your favorite piece of music? _____

ANSWERS: Please cut off this segment before photocopying. (1) 1685, 1759, 74; (2) Germany, France, Italy, London; (3) carriage, Katarina, 1759; (4) Handel, Duchess, Music Master, Keeper; (5) horses' hooves, rain, thunder, party talk, body thud, door opening, crickets; (6) "More people will come to see you jump than hear you sing," "Madame, you are welcome home," "Someday, I'll sprechen English besserer than you"; (7) his mother died, he is exploited by his Keeper, he cannot speak; (8) singing, of exhaustion and lack of food; (9) Katarina; (10) the 16th notes are too hard to sing; (11) she gets lost in the music; (12) in a garden; (13) her loss of Caesar; (14) he playfully imitates Madame Cuzzoni, he smiles at the monkeys in Handel's harpsichord, he almost reaches out for his mother at the opera, he joins Katarina practicing Messiah; (15) the announcement of the coming of Christ, the angels appearing and the joyful chorus; (16) his Keeper; (17) in the opera house; (18) singing to his spirit mother; (19) his mother can leave when Katarina and Handel welcome him into the Foundling School; (20) N/A; (21) N/A

Classical Kids Awards and Honors

Beethoven Lives Upstairs

AUDIO: Juno Award Best Children's Recording (Canada), Parents' Choice Silver Honor (U.S.), American Library Association Notable Children's Recording Award, Practical Home Schooling Reader Award Music Curriculum Category and Educational Audio Cassette Category (U.S.), Film Advisory Board Award of Excellence (U.S.), Parents' Choice Classic Award (U.S.), Certified Gold Record (Canada), Certified Platinum Record (Canada)

BOOK: Governor General's Award Finalist – Illustration (Canada), Canadian Children's Book Centre Our Choice Recommendation

VIDEO: Emmy Award for Best Children's Program, Parents' Choice Movie Hall of Fame Classic and Gold Awards (U.S.), Dove Foundation Dove Family Approved Seal, Oppenheim Toy Portfolio Platinum Award (U.S.), Film Advisory Board Award of Excellence (U.S.), Gold Camera Award Best Children's Program and Best Direction (U.S.), Certified Multi-Platinum Video (Canada)

CD-ROM: National Parenting Publications Honors Award (U.S.), Film Advisory Board Award of Excellence (U.S.), Curriculum Administrator Top 100 Districts' Choice Award (U.S.)

Mr. Bach Comes to Call

Parents' Choice Gold Award (U.S.), American Library Association Notable Children's Recording Award, Parents' Choice Classic Award (U.S.), Practical Home Schooling Reader Award Music Curriculum Category and Educational Audio Cassette Category (U.S.), Film Advisory Board Award of Excellence (U.S.), Certified Gold Record (Canada), Certified Platinum Record (Canada)

Tchaikovsky Discovers America

AUDIO: Juno Award Best Children's Recording (Canada), American Library Association Notable Children's Recording Award, Parents' Choice Classic Award (U.S.), Practical Home Schooling Reader Award Music Curriculum Category and Educational Audio Cassette Category (U.S.), Audio File Earphones Award of Excellence (U.S.), Certified Gold Record (Canada)

BOOK: Canadian Children's Book Centre Our Choice Recommendation, Gibbon Award Finalist Illustration (Canada)

Mozart's Magic Fantasy

Juno Award Best Children's Recording (Canada), Parents' Choice Gold Award, American Library Association Notable Children's Recording Award, Parents' Choice Classic Award (U.S.), Practical Home Schooling Reader Award Music Curriculum Category and Educational Audio Cassette Category (U.S.), Film Advisory Board Award of Excellence (U.S.), Certified Gold Record (Canada), Certified Platinum Record (Canada)

Vivaldi's Ring of Mystery

Juno Award Best Children's Recording (Canada), Parent's Choice Gold Award (U.S.), American Library Association Notable Children's Recording Award, Parents' Choice Classic Award (U.S.), Practical Home Schooling Reader Award Music Curriculum Category and Educational Audio Cassette Category (U.S.), Audio File Earphones Award of Excellence (U.S.), Film Advisory Board Award of Excellence (U.S.), Certified Gold Recording (Canada)

Daydreams & Lullabies

Film Advisory Board Award of Excellence (U.S.), Practical Home Schooling Reader Award Music Curriculum Category and Educational Audio Cassette Category (U.S.)

Hallelujah Handel!

Parent's Choice Gold Award (U.S.), Film Advisory Board Award of Excellence (U.S.), Practical Home Schooling Reader Award Music Curriculum Category and Educational Audio Cassette Category (U.S.)

Educational Awards

Curriculum Administrator Top 100 Districts' Choice Award, Learning Magazine – Teacher's Choice Award, Practical Home Schooling Association Notable Children's Recordings

The Classroom Collection

Teacher's Choice Award Learning Magazine

Susan Hammond, Classical Kids Producer

The Order of Canada for her contribution to arts and education in Canada